The Fearless Living Challenge:
A 49-Day Course To Living Your Greatness

by

Ericka D. Jackson

ISBN 978-1-4303-1374-8

Dedication

This book is dedicated to each and every client I have had the privilege of working with. Thank you for trusting me with your life, your challenges, and your willingness to be vulnerable. This work exists today because of you and you know who you are. From my very first days of wondering if I could really, truly help people transform their lives to now knowing the process inside and out. Every speaking engagement, every book, and every product exists because of our work together. I love you and I look forward to hearing the stories of your life.

Table of Contents

Welcome

Congratulations on being a part of this wonderful course! I am so excited to be able to usher you into fearless living. This is actually more than a course, it is a challenge or invitation to remove any remaining fear that has been holding you back or slowing you down. Since I have uncovered the powerful insights and techniques I will share with you during this course, my life and business have been "in the flow." When you are "in the flow" things begin to happen with divine synchronicity and God's favor is prevalent throughout your life and business.

As I sat and thought about the times in my life that fear has stopped or slowed me. Even before I truly understood the meaning and nature of fear, I realized that God has been preparing me my entire life to do this fearlessness work. I have always had some sort of inner knowing that has allowed me to move through fear. Of course, I have experienced it, but I always found a way to move forward in spite of my fear.

We all handle fear in different ways. When I

experienced fear, I handled it by stuffing it down with food. I guess I was trying to eat my way out of fear. Yes, I would keep moving forward, but I would eat half of the contents of the refrigerator in the process. Fear may show up for you in similar ways or in less obvious ways. Maybe you shop with money allocated for other expenses when you are in fear. Perhaps you get quiet and go into a shell. Maybe you just sit still, not moving forward enough to succeed or backward enough to fail.

No matter how you have handled fear in the past, this course will forever change how you will relate to fear. Fear of success, fear of failure, fear of the unknown, fear of rejection, fear of change, fear of being alone, fear of not having enough... Are you ready to leave fear behind once and for all!!?

Program Overview

I am very excited about this new, revolutionary offering that provides you with a focused plan that yields incredible results! You will learn how to fully walk, talk, breathe and think fearlessly. This challenge will call forth your fearless self!

After witnessing fear fall away from the lives of those I have worked closely with and learning how to transform fear into achievement in my own life, it is time to bring these teachings, insights, and techniques to you so we can walk fearlessly together. Imagine fear never slowing you down or stopping you again. Although it sounds impossible, this is how God designed you to live. In a moment of divine intervention, the truth about fear was revealed to me and I have been sharing it ever since (more about this in Challenge 2).

In this exciting 49-day course, my teachings, insights and loving support accompany you in breaking through your fear and *achieving* the boundless success.

In this wonderful course, I extend to you my 18 years of skill, expertise and spiritual gifts that The Lord has blessed me with in this proven step-by-step process. Here is an overview of what to expect so you can be fully prepared to maximize the power of this experience.

This course will cover:

Challenge 1: Designing Your Fearless Life
Challenge 2: The Truth About Fear
Challenge 3: Clearing The Way For Fearless

Living

Challenge 4: Releasing Emotional Barriers to Fearlessness

Challenge 5: Embracing Fearless Success

Challenge 6: Communicating Fearlessly To The World

Challenge 7: Walking In Your Greatness

This course will teach you the insights, tools and applications that will:

- Guide you in overcoming barriers to achieving your goals.

- Increase the reciprocity you experience in your relationships.

- Teach you how to open yourself up to receive all of God's goodness for your life.

- Increase your clarity on how to achieve your vision.

- Show you the steps to take daily toward living fearlessly.

- Assist you in communicating your truth, needs, and boundaries with love.

- Guide you in experiencing God on a deeper personal level.

What To Expect

The journey will be exciting, challenging, and at times uncomfortable. Anytime you move to new levels you will expand your comfort zones, explore limiting thoughts and beliefs, overcome past negative emotions, and challenge the bounds of your current reality. I have a different take on fear and you will hear new and different information about fear. Some concepts may be new to you and some may not. Be open. Everything that I teach is rooted deeply in spiritual truth and is scripturally-based (based on The Holy Bible). This is important because with so many spiritual beliefs out there in the world, you need to know that I deal only in The Holy Spirit and the work is safe to let the teachings into your spirit and allow it to do its work.

This work can be done no matter where you are in your spiritual walk or what your experience of religion has been. You may experience a variety of emotions, thoughts, and any remaining past limiting thoughts and beliefs will become illuminated just prior to you breaking through to fearlessness.

To best use this book, please read through it in its entirety one time without stopping to write your answers down. Then, choose a specific day to begin each Challenge. Each lesson will consist of teaching concepts, insights, questions for growth for you to explore and answer, and a homework assignment to apply the lesson for the week. Please make sure you take time between each Challenge to deepen your learning.

This book is provided for you to write and do the journaling that is necessary to move through this process. I invite you to challenge yourself to follow-through and play "big" during this process. This book contains the lessons, powerful questions, space for journaling, and a checklist of the week's homework lessons to complete.

Although you can complete your weekly assignments as your time permits, it is critical to set aside a specific time to complete each lesson. The key to successful completion is to schedule a time to complete the assignments each week. Mark your planner, add it to your Outlook calendar or program it into your electronic organizer. Whatever device or method you use, make it a reoccurring time for the next seven weeks.

Here is your first homework assignment:

Start thinking about the focus it will take to complete the Challenge within the 49 days. Which days will be your best homework days? What things might have to be put on hold in order to complete this challenge powerfully? Is there anything you can foresee standing in the way of completing this journey? Is fearlessness worth it?

How To Get The Most From This Experience

While the tools, lessons, and techniques are provided, there are some important things you bring forth to make the challenge a success:

- Focus
- Designated times to complete your homework assignments. Mark your planner, add it to your Outlook calendar or program it into your electronic calendar. Whatever system you use, make it a reoccurring appointment for the next 7 weeks.
- A willingness to confront your fears
- Shameless and honest truth-telling
- Trust the process. I've designed this as a step-by-step program and each step is critical to your success. Really take a week for each step, don't rush the process.

Definitions

Inquiry – A deep, probing question that takes time to ponder and answer.

Group Coaching Circles – A group of like-minded people focused on moving forward around a specific topic or area of focus. These occur on a tele-conference call line with others participating in the challenge. Please make sure you have signed up for my monthly e-zine on www.erickajackson.com so you can receive Coaching Circle announcements.

Powerful Question – A question posed to you that deepens your thought process, forwards your learning, and leaves you positively altered once you answer it.

Most of all, enjoy the process and stick with it no matter how uncomfortable it may become. I am here to support and encourage you throughout this journey.

The Fearless Living Challenge
Challenge 1: Designing Your Fearless Life

Challenge 1

Designing Your Fearless Life

This is the first week to 7 amazing weeks of your life! God has created you to live an extraordinary life. He has chosen you to stand out and be an example of what a blessed life looks like. He has promised you greatness. He has promised you wealth. He has promised to meet and exceed your needs so you can be a blessing to those around you. He has promised to bring you out of anything that has been holding you back from your "Promised Land."

When I think of the term, "Promised Land," I think of Dr. Martin Luther King's compelling speech he gave on April 3, 1968 in Memphis, Tennessee. While he was talking about the Promised Land that God has for African-American people, I want you to know that God has a Promised Land for you. In scripture, God tells of the Promised Land – the land of milk and honey, where your cup overflows and a table will be set for you. It is your destiny. It goes beyond dreaming of those things that are outside of you to knowing that what God has promised you is a seed that has been planted inside of you. It is already with you. Those things *will* take root and grow in time. It is inevitable.

Remember when you were a child and God revealed visions or glimpses of images of what was possible for your future? Remember the money He showed you you could have? You may have thought you were just fantasizing or dreaming about what you would like your life to be like. It was God giving you glimpses of what He has for you. No one can get your blessing. It has your name written on it and only you hold the key to unlocking it. It is time to remember your Promised Land.

You may seldom get to talk about your Promised Land in a way people can really hear you and truly be happy for you. You may share parts of it, but treat other aspects of it as if it is top secret. It's time to let it out. Take all of your childhood dreams, your adolescent imaginings, and adult-desires, goals, and longings and there you have your

Promised Land. Instead of reducing your dream or Promised Land to fit into your life, we will stretch your life to the size of your Promised Land.

This Week's Focus: This week of the

challenge is all about you deciding how you choose to experience this challenge and what you will get out of this process. So much of your fear is about not knowing what it will look like on the "other side" of fear. Well, this is your chance to define and articulate it so you will naturally allow it to manifest in your life.

Take those visions in which God has given you that have shown you bits and pieces of what is to come. Add a helping of what you know you are capable of and a heaping spoon full of your deepest desires and there you have it. Right there, in front of you is what you not only choose your life to look like, but what is promised to you. For a moment, allow yourself to forget about the "how" and just focus on the promise.

Have you seen yourself traveling to exotic places feeling relaxed (which means the money, time, business, etc, is handled)? Have you seen yourself with an incredible life partner who adores you and honors you? Have you seen yourself at a certain body size? Have you seen yourself connecting with movers and shakers and speaking in front of rooms full of people that came to hear you speak? Have you seen yourself working with clients to teach them how to love themselves and transform their worlds? What is it?

Before the circumstances of your life changed, what did you envision for your future? Don't hold back. What does it look like? What is the pinnacle of what you know God has for you? Paint me a picture of your promised land. What is your promised land? It is time to articulate your promised land.

Use this space to write out a detailed description of your promised land (use the back of this sheet if you need to):

_____

_____

_____

_____

_____

_____

This Week's Exercises

❏ Complete your written description of your promised land.

❏ Continue opening yourself up to your promised land and continue writing about it throughout the week.

❏ Focus on it being real; not a dream or desires stuck in your imagination. Practice allowing your promised land to be as real to you as the air you breathe and as normal and familiar to you as the beating of your heart. Inhale it. Close your eyes often and see it. Taste it. *Feel it.*

❏ Share it with at least one person that has the capacity to "get" it. If you don't have someone in your life in this role, let me be that person for you. Email it to me at info@erickajackson.com and I'll hold your space of greatness for you.

❏ Complete the below Powerful Questions & Inquiries.

Powerful Questions & Inquiries

There are a few powerful questions that you will need to take the time to answer this week in order to uncover the ways you have held onto your fear. Take a deep breath and access your inner truth and honesty. I may ask you a question that sounds similar to previous questions, but it is designed to uncover a different level or inner dimension. Trust the process and take time to answer it. Use the back of your page if you need to, but let it flow...

As you look back over your life, what has fear held you back from? Take this space to write your reflections.

_____

_____

_____

_____

_____

_____

What would you have done differently if you had no fear?

_____

_____

_____

_____

_____

_____

_____

_____

_____

How has being fearful served you? What has been in it for you? What has fear allowed you to hide from?

_____

_____

_____

_____

_____

_____

_____

_____

How has fear shown up in your life? How you have handled your fear? (Some stuff theirs down with food, some just don't move, some hide behind things or people, etc....)

_____

_____

_____

_____

_____

_____

_____

_____

_____

Why are you willing to let your fear go?

_____

_____

_____

_____

_____

_____

_____

_____

_____

The Fearless Living Challenge
Challenge 2: The Truth About Fear

Challenge 2

The Truth About Fear

Six years ago, I walked away from my stifling corporate job as an Administrative Recruiter (I think they gave me some fancy title, but that was the gist of it) to honor my deep desire. Knowing that it was time to live God's purpose full-time. I began putting together a Professional Coaching business that would one day become a world-class speaking and training institute. About three years into building my business, it was time to make the transition into speaking, my true gift, as my major income stream. In preparation for this I was doing market research on other speakers and professional coaches. As I read website after website, it became evident that they were all saying the same things. We were using the same words to describe our work and the outcomes we delivered. I took a deep breath and realized I had gone as far as I could without having the clarity and walking in the knowing of what made me unique as a speaker and coach.

Although my business was growing, it was coming together much slower than I had predicted on my Sales Forecasts. My cash flow kept me struggling and I was feeling a panicked fear about the future of my business. I sat there quietly at my two-tiered Ikea pressboard desk that I'd stayed up until 3:30am one morning to assemble, and asked myself, "What makes me different from all the others?" Nothing extraordinary was coming to mind.

As I looked around at the 500 square-foot, one bedroom, apartment my 7 year-old daughter and I had lived in for more than a year to minimize my expenses so I could keep growing my business, I just knew I *had* to "get" this in order to move out of this miniscule apartment and on to my dreams. I was at the end of what I knew to do. I asked God, "God, what makes me different than the others you have called to similar work?"

The next voice I heard was not my own. This voice came from within my spirit and said, "I have put all of the answers within my children and they are not being obedient. Your job is to help them be obedient to my call. If they will heed my call, the world will be transformed." I then saw images of famine, starving children, homelessness, poverty, and inner city crime flash through my mind.

Then the voice of God continued by saying, "I have put the answers to all of the world's problems in my children, if only they will be obedient. Your job is to help my children be obedient." From that day on, my fear disappeared and I deeply and profoundly understood my specific calling and purpose in this world. I have been heeding God's call to be a catalyst to guide God's children in full obedience with His call on their lives ever since.

About a year later, I was planning the lesson for the Teen Sunday School class I had taught for years at First AME Church in Seattle, Washington. I was preparing a lesson on fear, and as I was reading the Word about fear I noticed it was used in several different contexts. I needed a deeper understanding to be able to teach my students. I then asked The Lord, "I have read your Word and I am not clear about fear. Please reveal to me the truth about fear." In just moments, my reply came and said, "Fear is the lack of surrender or submission to God."

Wow! What!? I applied that definition and re-read the passages in the Word about fear and it fit! That was it! *Fear is the lack of surrender or submission to God.* I have been teaching it ever since and it has fit for everyone I have shared it with. Did you get it? *This* is the truth about fear. It is so important that you understand this; it is the cornerstone of this course. Here it is again...

Fear is the lack of surrender or submission to God.

This Week's Focus: This week is all

about understanding the truth about fear. My intention is to open up the gates of your understanding and clarity so you can deeply understand the nature of fear and how to use your past fear as guides to light your way to your promised land.

There are institutes, classes, workshops, and books solely dedicated to the topic of fear. My vision for this course is that it is the last course you will ever need. Once you understand the truth about fear, you can get on with the business of bringing forth the incredible vision that God has planted in you.

To move forward, you must also understand what fear is not - it is not False Evidence Appearing Real. This is the definition of fear I have seen over and over again and it is not fully accurate. I felt like I would scream if I saw this definition in another book or heard another speaker refer to it.

As I was reading a book day-before-yesterday, there it was again - False Evidence Appearing Real. I did actually let out a frustrated scream. My daughter heard me from her upstairs bedroom and called out, "Mommy, what's wrong?!" I yelled back, "Nothin," but the truth is that we have to stop perpetuating this untruth about fear because it keeps us operating out of our egos and not our spirits – the realm in which fear exists.

You must understand the spiritual nature of fear and use spiritual tools, or tools from God, to guide your way through fear. Fear is not something just in your mind. Fear is not just doubt or your negative thoughts. Fear is a spiritual issue and simply cannot be reckoned with in your mind, your will, or your ego.

You may have been taught that fear is your

enemy and you can fight it. You may have believed until now that you can affirm or attempt to overcome your fear with positive self-talk and cute affirmations posted on your bathroom mirror. You cannot ever affirm your way out of fear. Affirmations will help for a minute, but your fear will come up again shortly and take hold of you.

Perhaps you have been trying to push or move forward in spite of your fear. Fear is the way you can monitor the spiritual doors through which darkness enters your thoughts, habits, and life. Fear illuminates the areas of your life in which you do not believe God will provide for you. The opposite of fear is faith. Fear and faith cannot co-exist. You have to choose one or the other. Once you believe God for that particular thing you feared before, it no longer has a stronghold on you and the spirit of fear will find somewhere else to reside. Removing fear from your life is the doorway to your will and God's will for you becoming one.

Now that you are clear about the true meaning and purpose of fear, it's time to take a good look at your life and identify the type of fear(s) you are facing. You may think of fear as one, big, insurmountable mountain and haven't taken much time to see what the mountain is made of. Without knowing what your mountain of fear is comprised of, you will not be able to dismantle your fear very easily. Let's take a look at the main types of fear. As you read these, make note of which ones are real for you right now. The main types of fear are:

1. Fear of being alone
2. Fear of not being or feeling loved
3. Fear of loss of privacy or the "fishbowl"
4. Fear of increased responsibility
5. Fear of being exposed
6. Fear of not having enough
7. Physical fears or phobias (spiders, snakes, etc.)

Fear of Being Alone

Cindy is a 5'1", curvaceous, vivacious one-time actress involuntarily turned administrative recruiter who was the life of the party wherever she went. Whether she's working at the desk of her corporate job, or flinging her naturally curly red hair over her shoulder as she grooves on the dance floor, she is a ball of energy that will keep you roaring with laughter.

I met Cindy about 8 years ago when I first

started working in administrative staffing. Although we unknowingly picked a horrible employer, Cindy would brighten any day with her jokes and light-hearted way of dealing with people at her Temp employment desk.

It didn't take long for me to see through her comedic veneer to her insecurity and fear of being by herself. I first noticed when she showed me a picture of Peter, the man she had been dating. Cindy often complained about the snide and rude comments Peter would make to her. He was nice and loving in one moment and for some reason, unbeknownst to her, he would turn derogatory and negative toward her in the next moment.

Peter was a pale, pasty man with a receding hairline and a belly that had long since expanded over his beltline. I remember trying to hide the look of shock on my face when she showed me this picture of the "love of her life." Even in the picture, I could sense his insecurity and desire to inflict his pain on those around him.

Cindy and I remained friends after I left that staffing agency. Two years later she hired me as her success coach. We spent quite a bit of time helping her remember her greatness and uncover her calling. She began spending more time alone and learned to appreciate and love herself. She stopped using her sense of humor as a mask for her pain and began expressing it as an art form. She was obedient to her coaching assignments of researching area theater auditions and working with an acting coach. Peter became threatened by her new-found confidence. Her current circle of friends, who were Peter's friends first, also realized that their negative, unsupportive comments no longer found life with Cindy.

During one of our coaching sessions, she proudly declared, "I have found myself and I really like who I am! I don't need Peter or anyone else who does not like me for who I am. I would rather not be with anyone right now and just focus on myself." Yes! This is a coach's dream moment. As her coach, I saw it from the very beginning, but I had to guide her to her own inner understanding, spirituality and breakthrough.

She released her fear of being alone and learned to walk in faith, believing God has a man chosen just for her. Cindy is now happily engaged to a wonderful man who supports her acting and loves her colorful personality. They are building their dream home with a view of Lake Washington and will be moving in soon. She regularly performs improv around the region, is working on her own one-woman-show and loves her life.

Fear of Not Being or Feeling Loved

I just have to share my story on this one. When I first decided to start my own business, the first thing I did was hire a success coach. I found Jennifer, a wonderful coach and we connected instantly. The first thing we had to move through was my fear of being on my own in business. During one of our many powerful coaching sessions she asked me, "Ericka, what are you afraid of? What is your biggest fear about moving forward?"

I sat there for a moment really trying to access my truth and then I felt a lump in my throat and felt my mouth go dry. I had found my answer, "I'm afraid that no man will be able to handle me. I've always been told that I intimidate men and if I intimidate them now, they really won't be able to handle me when I'm living my dream life. I'm scared that I will never have the love I want to experience." Tears started rolling down my cheeks as we sat there on the phone and just let the depth of that comment sink in.

She offered me a reframe and asked me, "Ericka, is there another way you can look at this that will reflect what you really want?"

"Yes, I can choose to know that working my business and living my vision will lead me to the man God has created for me. "

"Yes," she said in her calming voice that had a way of helping me delve into the deepest parts of myself.

Before that coaching moment, I had chosen to believe that being successful would mean that I would never have the love I do deeply desire. I changed my mind that day. I decided that living my vision was the only way to cross paths with a man that can handle all of who I was and all I am striving to be. I was able to release my fear of not being or feeling loved that day. I am absolutely clear and faithful that God is bringing the man He intends for me. Ever since that day, I have built my vision knowing that each day I am closer to my divine partner. I'll let you know when he arrives. But, until then, I have no fear around that and I know that I know he is coming soon and in perfect timing.

Fear of Loss of Privacy or The "Fishbowl"

The challenge of visionaries is that our work is public and when we are operating in our calling, many around the city, country, nation, and world will notice. You probably have an inherent knowing that stepping into the fullness of your calling will touch many, many lives and you may be holding back because you are harboring fear of people peering into every aspect of your life. Although you have to be aware of your choices, you can actually create increased privacy when you live your vision.

I actually had to work with this as a fear of mine. As my work was getting out more and more, I was experiencing people recognizing me in Seattle and watching me very closely. Although it was only happening several times a week, I realized that I am a very private person and was resisting putting my work out even more powerfully. This fear along with my gift of feeling what other people feel can make being in crowds a real challenge for me. I audibly hear the issues, challenges and feel the emotional pain of others. Once I released this fear to God, I began spending time with friends who had plenty of money and I found that they were a part of a more exclusive world of private box seats and exclusive membership clubs that included private dining and paying monthly tabs.

About two months before I moved from Seattle, I remember one busy holiday weekend. My friend Jeanette and I wanted to go out to dinner. We drove past The Cheesecake Factory and saw a huge crowd of people waiting to be seated. While others were circling the block for street parking, Jeanette and I parked her navy blue Chevrolet Trailblazer at The Washington Athletic Club in the heart of downtown Seattle.

While every restaurant in the city was packed and had lines of people waiting hours to be seated, we headed to the exclusive restaurant in The Washington Athletic Club – better known as "The WAC" – and were seated immediately in their wonderful restaurant. The meal was delectable and there were only one or two other parties in the restaurant. We had impeccable service and attention. At that moment, I realized that working my vision would afford me these wonderful experiences, and I could protect my privacy and better manage when I choose to be around crowds of people.

Fear of Increased Responsibility

How many times have your heard, "To whom much is given, much is required?" It is scriptural as well as wisdom that has been passed on from generation to generation. I hear this fear most often associated with getting finances in order. I also see this fear in action when God is calling you to move to new levels in leadership, career or business. This fear is a very subtle fear and takes some soul-searching to recognize. It often comes up when God is calling you to a higher post and leads to fear of not being good enough or having enough skill to pull off your new position or placement.

This fear can also come up as you move your business to new areas of exposure and acquire more ideal clients. Although you get what you said you wanted, it can often lead to experiencing this fear. Know that this is a normal part of expanding your work and getting your work out into the world. It is a good sign that you are moving in the right direction. With your new understanding of fear and how to alleviate it, you don't have to be stuck in your current comfort zone.

Fear of Being Exposed

There is another kind of fear that may be keeping you from living your dreams. I grew up reading *Essence* magazine and actually had a collection of Susan L. Taylor's *In the Spirit* columns that were in the front of every issue. Living in an all-white area with very little that told me that I was attractive and worthy, I cleaved to Susan's articles and always felt uplifted and a little closer to who God intended me to be after I read her work. When I transferred from Western Washington University in Bellingham, Washington to Howard University in Washington, DC, one day on campus, I saw a pink flier with Susan's picture saying she was speaking at The University of Maryland. I knew I couldn't miss it.

As I walked into the unassuming classroom, I was surprised at how quaint the gathering was and I got a chance to sit in the front row as she described her deep insecurities about not having a formal undergraduate education. At the time, *Essence* had moved into television and chose Susan as a host for their interview-format program. Her tall, slender, fit stature stood behind a table-top podium and as her beautifully manicured fingers rested effortlessly on the edge of the podium, she stood and described in her elegant, thoughtful way the terror she would experience knowing she was interviewing well-read, well-educated people.

She shared that she felt like her lack of formal college education and degree would be found out. While her face and questions masked her fear, she felt like she would be exposed for her lack of formal educational training and people would see her as a fake. Eventually she had enough and she pursued her formal college education in spite of being in her 30's.

You may be living with a fear of something in your past being exposed or someone from your past coming back to haunt you just as you step out in to the world to bring your vision to the masses. Again, because fear is a spiritual issue, only God can deal with it. Surrender it and know that God will always take care of you, one of his most precious children.

Fear of Not Having Enough

Can you believe I almost forgot this major

fear? I had to go back and add it to the list. This should actually be the first fear on the list because it is the one that keeps most people from living God's vision and stepping out on faith. Fear of not having enough time, privacy, friends, energy, money, sleep, clients, cash flow, resources...it can go on and on. I've learned that the fear of not having enough money has kept more people bound than any other.

It's easy to talk about trusting that God will provide for you in theory, but when it comes to really stepping out of your comfort zone to start your business or organization, it becomes much more challenging to actually move on your fear. I have learned that the more faith you have in God, the more He will provide for you when you give your life and livelihood to His work.

After my daughter and I moved out of our tiny 500 square-foot, "temporary" apartment that we lived in for three years, we moved into a two-bedroom mother-in-law bungalow on the property of The Gray family. Marvin is the father of the wonderful family whose property we lived on until we moved to the East coast.

Marvin is a Minister and served as the youth pastor of his church. He is passionate and gifted in working with inner-city youth and helping them overcome their pasts to create powerful futures. About one year after we moved in, Marvin shared with me that his church was eliminating his position and he was looking for employment.

I clearly saw that Marvin is called to have his own international youth ministry. He already had the contacts and his work was known in the circles of national inner city youth ministries. I shared this with him one evening in a late-night email. He replied that although it sounded great, he needed to make sure he brought in at least $3000 a month to feed his four kids and wife.

I remember thinking and trying to share with him that if He would step out on faith, God would take care of him. Even as a Pastor, he was challenged with really trusting God to provide more than enough money for his family to live on while he lived his Vision.

Instead, in response to his difficulty in getting a job and needing to provide for his family, he decided to buy a 1976, blue Ford pick-up truck and clean gutters. While the work kept him busy, I noticed sadness come over Marvin that broke my heart. I saw the bright sparkle in his eyes diminish to a mere flicker of light.

I knew it was part of his process of learning to trust God with his livelihood, but it was hard for me to watch when I saw clearly what God has for him. I still pray that he steps out on faith and commits to living God's vision so he can get his joy back and his family can see faith in action as God provides for their needs and desires. I can't help but imagine where his life would be if he had been willing to believe God for the finances he and his family needed to live comfortably. God will provide for you when you put forth the work of living His purpose and be obedient to the calling on your life.

Physical Fears or Phobias (Spiders, Snakes, Etc.)

I am actually chuckling to myself and I write this because for the last three weeks, the largest spider I have ever seen has taken up residence on my back porch. Normally, I would have taken something to destroy her web and force her to go elsewhere. But, this particular spider was the size of the palm of my hand and being in a new city, I had never seen this type of black spider with yellow markings on its body.

One day I even worked up the nerve to head out to the porch to encourage it to go away. I don't like killing bugs and I usually just catch them in an old jar and let them go in the bushes, but this one was different. I named her Charlotte and I feared that Charlotte could jump on me or that she was big enough to capture me and put me into my spder-catching jar.

I checked daily to see if Charlotte was still there. After three weeks, I still had not worked up the nerve to go near her. Then the day I looked out there and saw that she had built a nest, I decided enough was enough. I remembered the truth about fear and decided to see if I could apply the same principles and steps to getting this giant spider off of my back porch. I prayed to God and asked Him to have that spider leave my back porch. The next morning she was gone and I have not seen her since.

When I began this work, I thought that physical phobias followed a different set of rules. I have since learned that fear is fear. When you believe God will protect you and provide for you, even physical phobias fall away from your life. Whether you are afraid of snakes, mice, water, driving, darkness, heights, or critters of any kind, God will protect you. Walk in your authority above things in the physical world and your fear will cease to have a hold on you.

The Manifestations of Fear

There are many ways that fear can show up in your life. Ways you may not have identified as fear because they were not obvious. Recognizing how you interact with fear is very powerful because it allows you to remove it in all of its forms. The five main ways fear subtly manifests are:

1. Procrastination/never trying
2. Over Eating
3. Over Spending
4. Doubt
5. Staying too busy

Which subtle ways do fear show up in your life?

_____

_____

_____

_____

_____

How To Surrender Your Fear

As you begin this process of alleviating your fear, fear will still be a part of your reality. Your current fears are tools that you will use to move beyond your fear. In other words, God allows fear for a very healthy reason – so you can always be aware of the areas in which you don't believe Him. Without fear, you would have no barometer to tell you when you are "off." Fear can serve as guiding lights to illuminate those things and areas of your life that you have not yet surrendered.

When you experience fear, the steps to making it disappear are:

1. Confess your fear(s).
2. Remember what God has promised you.
3. Identify what you are not believing God for.
4. Imagine what it would be like without the fear.
5. Pray the Prayer of Surrender (below).

Now that you know the steps to take to surrender your fear, we have to talk about understanding and activating God's favor in your life. Favor is just that, receiving preferential treatment or having special attention. Being a child of God entitles you to experience God's favor and covering. This favor and covering provides you with some important benefits that non-believers do not have access to. This favor is activated once you give your spirit and soul to God through being "saved." Being saved gives you access into an elite membership club of individuals that are actively (in an ideal world, people wouldn't be so jacked-up around spirituality and religion) striving to be closer to God on a daily and weekly basis.

The Prayer of Surrender

This is a sample prayer that you can pray to alleviate your fear. Change words, phrases, and sentences to something that feels natural and real for you. This is just a template for you to build upon.

Dear Heavenly Father,

I thank you and praise you for all you are and all you are doing in my life. Thank you for being such an awesome and mighty God. Lord, I thank you for the many, many blessings you have bestowed upon me. I thank you for every triumph and challenge I have experienced that leads me closer to you. Lord, I confess that I am experiencing fear. I am fearful about _____ and I know that in order to move forward, it is time to release this fear. Lord, I have done all that I know to do and I am asking for your help.

I know that all things are possible through Christ who strengthens me. I am standing in my power as your child and I release this fear right now. I surrender this fear to you, God, and call forth _____, in the name of Jesus. Lord, I am asking for a miracle and in order to live your vision, I ask you for _____. I thank you for fulfilling my every need and providing all that I need to live your will. All this I pray in Jesus' name, Amen.

Powerful Questions & Inquiries

What are your current fears?

_____

_____

_____

_____

_____

_____

_____

_____

In what areas do you procrastinate or doubt? List everything you have been procrastinating on in your life:

_____

_____

_____

_____

_____

_____

_____

In what ways has your fear held you back, slowed you down, or kept you stuck?

_____

_____

_____

_____

_____

_____

What other ways do you mask or hide your fear?

_____

_____

_____

_____

_____

_____

_____

_____

_____

In what ways have you sabotaged yourself or abused yourself because of fear?

_____

_____

_____

_____

_____

_____

_____

_____

This week's exercises

- Complete your Powerful Questions & Inquiries for this week.

- Take a look at your list of fears (procrastinations and doubts), and ask yourself, "Will I believe God for this?" or "Am I willing to fully surrender this and believe it is working out for my highest good?"

- Tweak your Prayer of Surrender in a way that works for you and begin saying it to yourself every morning in your devotion and quiet time.

- Read the following Favor Confession.
  Since I have moved to Raleigh, NC, I have found the most incredible church experience I have ever had. My experience proves that this is no small feat because I have attended churches that are filled with deception, negativity, judgment, arrogance, and frightened people.

My previous church did not keep proper financial records and it was uncovered that more than $500,000 was embezzled by someone who was well known in the community. It has been a challenge for me to be a part of organized religion and not allow our human frailties, shortcomings, misuse of power, and lack of the true experience of living God's word to cloud my ability to focus on God.

I am now at a church where I feel absolutely free to live God's word. I literally run to attend Bible Study and Church every Wednesday and Sunday. Last week at church, I noticed an unassuming piece of goldenrod paper with some words typed on it stapled to a plain cork bulletin board. I stopped and actually took a closer look at those words and was blown away at the power of what they said. It was entitled, *Favor Confession*. It has no author or dates on it. I stood there and read the words and my mouth dropped at their power, authority, and expectation.

I realize that favor is really the next level beyond fear. Surrendering the fear ushers you into a realm few ever experience in life – the realm of walking in your God-given favor. On Wednesday night as my Pastor, Jeffery Chapman, Sr., closed out

Bible Study I snuck out a bit early and stood in the back hallway long enough to copy this *Favor Confession* for you. I'm not sure who wrote it, but I knew I had to share it with you. I am intentionally putting this on a page of its own so you can print it up and post it in a place that will remind you to walk in God's glory each and every day. I am getting in the habit of reciting it every morning during my prayer and meditation time. I hope to say it so much that I soon have it memorized. I invite you to do the same. Enjoy!

Favor Confession

Father, thank you for making me righteous and accepted through the blood of Jesus. Because of that, I am blessed and highly favored by you. I am the object of your affection. Your favor surrounds me as a shield and the first thing that people come into contact with is my shield.

Thank you that I have favor with you and man today. All day long, people go out of their way to bless and to help me. I will have favor with everyone that I deal with today. Doors that were once closed are now opened for me. I receive preferential treatment and I have special privileges. I am God's favored child.

No good thing will He withhold from me. Because of God's favor, my enemies cannot triumph over me. I have supernatural increase and promotion. I declare restoration of everything that the devil has stolen from me. I have honor in the midst of my adversaries and an increase of assets – especially in real estate and an expansion of territory.

Because I am highly favored by God, I experience great victories, supernatural turn-rounds and miraculous breakthroughs in the midst of great impossibilities. I receive recognition, prominence, and honor. Even ungodly authorities grant petitions to me. Policies, rules, regulations, and laws are changed and reversed on my behalf.

I win battles that I don't even have to fight because God fights them for me. This is the day, the set time and the designated moment for me to experience the free favors of God that profusely and lavishly abound on my behalf.

In Jesus' Name, Amen. ~~~

Isn't that amazing? Keep stating it out loud and practicing it and like anything you do over and over again, it will become part of you and call forth the powerful wonders of God daily for you and your business.

The Fearless Living Challenge
Challenge 3: Clearing The Way For Fearless Living

Challenge 3

Clearing The Way For

Fearless Living

Now that you have conceived what your life will look like without fear and you understand the truth about fear and how it has been showing up in your life, it's time to clear away anything and everything that stands in the way of living the life God has chosen for you. I know you are ready; we just have a bit of housekeeping to handle.

One of the questions I hear more often than any other is, "Where Do I Begin?" You see, knowing your kingdom assignment is not enough. It is only the beginning of the journey. In order to move to new levels, you must first prepare your life for vision by releasing and removing a few things to make your path straight.

This week is where your seriousness about living your vision will be challenged. You can actually stay busy everyday for the rest of your life without ever making a significant impact in your area of purpose. It is so easy to think about, plan, talk about, and write the goals of achieving your vision.

Doing each of these things already sets you apart from many others who aren't even thinking in terms of their vision and it's easy to get comfortable. But it's not enough for you. You are a doer and an achiever. You just need to make sure your life is set up in a way that fully supports your vision work.

This Week's Focus: This week is about handling the details of your physical environment, unprofitable or negative habits, and areas that are crying out for order. This week you will discern the areas that need attention as you take your business and life to new levels.

Right about now, you may be experiencing a heavy feeling on your shoulders, or your stomach may be doing flips because your life will never be the same. While this is true, the path to God's vision has many dimensions. You will laugh. You will cry. You will be challenged. You will connect with some incredible people heading in the same direction.

While you should take this work seriously, it is a simple process – not easy, but simple. God has laid out a step-by-step plan for you. It is about taking baby steps every single day, in the midst of others who are standing still or moving backward. When you do this, you will look back after a week, month, or year and be amazed at how far you have come.

The Power of Order

I no longer rely on my ego or mind to create my new product and service offerings or think up what to do next in my business. I actually pray and ask God for the next topics or offerings. I recently did this and was "told" to do a teleclass on *Creating Order: How to Grow Your Vision Without Feeling Overwhelmed*. When God gave me this topic, I was thinking of order in terms of physical cleaning, organizing, or de-cluttering. I soon learned God had something else in mind as I was preparing for the teleclass.

As I was reading scripture about order, my understanding of the importance of order moved to a whole new level. I already understood that God blesses order and dis-order holds up your blessings. I also knew that there is a correct order to things in our lives. I've also learned something new. I learned that order is a doorway to your blessings.

Order opens the doorway to your blessings.

There are three main contexts in which order is used in The Bible. Order is used to describe a certain process of carrying out commands from a higher authority or the reign of a king; order is used to describe the family succession of relatives or siblings; and order is used as a gateway to receive God's blessings.

In the last context, there is always an instruction and then the words, "in order to..." followed by the blessing that implementing that order will lead to. I realized that I could substitute the words, "and as a result" for order. My mouth fell open as I realized that honoring order opens the door to mighty blessings in your life. Do you see it? Please make sure you really get this. Read it again and again until the understanding permeates your mind and spirit. Order is the doorway to blessings and increase.

Order is not an action, it is a state of mind. Organization is a natural result of an ordered mind. Order is about having authority in every area of your life – from your closets, to your checkbook. Where there is dis-order, you are not walking in your God-given authority and dominion.

This Week's Focus: This week is all

about taking dominion over every area of your life. You may be saying to yourself, "That sounds great, but I don't have time to stop and think about all of this right now," or "Why do I have to have full order when no one will really know?" That's the challenge of living with areas of your life in disorder (trust me, I am working on this one, too!). Disorder usually occurs in the areas no one sees on a regular basis. It occurs in those areas you can tuck behind something or that don't directly affect people too quickly if it is not handled.

That closet, your finances, your marriage, your dresser drawer or your goals are all areas that may be out of order, but no one will really see these areas. Perhaps your business contacts are not in order. Maybe your closets are not in order. Perhaps your eating habits are not in order. Maybe you have been so focused on building your business and getting new clients that you haven't focused on keeping your finances in order and your financial entries are three months behind and your receipts are in your wallet, checkbook, that little space in your dashboard, or in different bags depending on which one you had when you acquired the receipt.

While you don't have to stop everything to get 100% order in your life, you do need to work on it enough to make sure you can move forward powerfully and purposefully. Even though the topic of order can feel heavy, it doesn't have to be. Just keep it light, take baby-steps and know that whatever state the interior of your life is in, it has gotten you this far and you've been able to work wonders. Most of all, remember to just laugh at it, because when your vision manifests, you can pay someone to handle all of that.

This preparation phase is the tedious part of building your vision. While imagining the fullness of your vision can come quickly, the manifestation takes time, so be patient and be present to every step in the journey because there is learning in each step. Enjoy the process and remember that the destination is inevitable if you follow the following steps to prepare the way.

Getting Your World Ready For Fearless Living

There are many ways to sabotage yourself from getting what you say you really want. I am fully aware of just how good I am at sabotaging myself. My self-sabotage shows up by not getting enough rest (I'm usually on the phone with friends wayyyy too late at night), eating foods that do a number on my body (I KNOW I need to stay away from the sugar because my body just can't handle it like it used to), and not keeping on top of my day-by-day finances (keeping my QuickBooks up to date, filing my receipts, etc.).

You may have a list of goals or desires you would love to achieve, yet most live your vision "on the side." It is because the way is not unobstructed for vision. The difference between you and people who cannot convert their dreams to reality is that they have not properly prepared their world and environment. Here is a checklist and explanations of things to be working on to assist you in moving forward fearlessly:

❏ Make space on your plate

A mistake that is easy for you to make as you expand your life to live fearlessly is trying to add more onto an already full plate. Make your vision a priority in your life and not allowing anything or anyone to get in the way. Take a good look at everything on your calendar and your current commitments and obligations.

Include things you may not think are negotiable including that church committee you volunteer on, the activities you run your children to and from, the friendships that keep you up on the phone past your bedtime, the grocery shopping you do every week, the role you may have in the family business, etc.

Take a look at each one and ask yourself, "Does this forward my vision?" or "Can I put this on the back burner until my vision is closer to being a reality?" You must create time for your vision in order to move forward.

❒ Body/Vessel – the vision is only as good as the vessel

This one took me years to figure out! In the first years of building my business, I took horrible care of my body, thinking I should sacrifice my well-being for God's vision. Then, after looking at myself with sacks – actually mine are more like bags - under my eyes, watching my hips grow even wider, and trying to operate through the fog of staying up every night until 2:00 a.m. or 3:00 a.m., God gave me much insight on this area.

Since your body is your temple, you must take even better care of it as a visionary because your body is the vessel through which the vision is birthed. If you are tired, your vision shows up tired. If you are unhealed, your vision comes through as broken. If you are overweight, your vision does not manifest as powerfully as it would through a physically fit body. If you are on dialysis, your vision is on dialysis. Your vision is only as good as the vessel. Make taking care of your vessel or body a priority. A great place to begin is by getting enough sleep. You will operate more effectively and find your energy will increase and lead the way for other changes in your life.

❏ Family

This is a tough one to talk about and distinguish from vision because so much of your vision is tied to your family. Perhaps part of your inspiration to making your vision a reality is that your children will live better lives. Maybe you strive for things because it will increase household income or your parents have come to expect it from you. Yet, your family can keep you bound.

Wait – before you dismiss this one as not being an issue, really take a deep breath and ask yourself, "Are the roles I play in my family forwarding my vision or hindering my vision from manifesting?" Is there anything you are willing to do to change this? This is a deep one and might need some additional attention.

❏ Relationships/Friendships

From Zig Ziglar to Les Brown, motivational speakers have talked and talked about the power of surrounding yourself with people who are positive, supportive and are also working toward their vision. Yet you may still find yourself nursing along emotionally needy friends, lending an ear to a mother who supports you only some of the time and then says something scathing to you in the name of love. Maybe your significant other is threatened by your vision because it requires you to meet new people and spend more time away from home.

Whatever the case with your friendships and significant relationship, it is important to take notice of how much energy they contribute or take from your vision. If you find they are taking more than they give, begin thinking of what will work for you as you move forward. I will cover the art of communicating your vision in Challenge Six. Until then, just be thinking about what you really need to feel supported, energized and surrounded by those who inspire and encourage you.

I really had to make some changes in my friendships when I fully committed to living my vision. I shaved back the time I spent talking to people that did not reciprocate the energy and enthusiasm I brought to the friendship. I also had to let go of those who held me on a pedestal and waited for me to reach out to them. I spent less time doing coffee with acquaintances and being on the phone with everyone who called me to chat.

I am now taking it to a new level and consciously spending a majority of my time with other business owners, because of their respect for time and their understanding of what it takes to be successful in business and the world. It's time to take inventory of the friendships and relationships that work for you and release those that no longer fit who you are and where you are going.

☐ Time

I already mentioned how easy it is to stay busy around the clock without having time to focus in on achieving your vision. God has deposited within you the image of what your life is supposed to look like and it is up to you to figure out how to manage your time to make it happen. Time is your most valuable asset in vision-land. Time is also the one thing that we all have equally. While some business owners have more resources or capital and some have more expertise or experience than others, you have the same 24 hours a day to execute. The most important aspects of success – focus, determination, planning, positivity, tenacity, patience, and persistence – do not cost a single penny. While I have an entire course just on time management and don't have the space or time to outline it here, in this book, here are some keys to help you master your time:

1. Practice the golden rule of time.

Slow down to get more done.

This sounds like an oxymoron, but it is so true. Slow down to be more thorough and follow through to completion.

2. Routines. Develop routines that work for you in both the morning and evening. Also develop routines for specific days of the week, while still leaving time for heeding God's direction on a daily basis.

3. Foresight. Take time to plan out your day and your week ahead of time. Spend some time on Sunday plotting out your week and identifying projects and tasks you will complete. Spend some time at the end of your work day or before you go to bed planning the next day's projects and tasks.

4. Office hours. Set clear, concise and consistent visionary office hours daily and work them better than you would a part-time job. These hours are dedicated hours to focus in without the phone, people or email disturbing you. Make sure you post the hours so people around you know what to expect and how to support you during this time.

5. Outgoing first. Before you open your email inbox, check the mail or check your messages, send out all messages, make all phone calls and send out correspondence first so you don't end up taking timely detours that lead you down a path you did not expect to go. Detours cost you valuable time and energy.

6. Group tasks. This is a basic time-management tip that still stands the test of time. With foresight, you can group like tasks and the time you have to complete them. Other than going to the post office three different times during the week, pick a day and take all of your correspondence on that day. Choose chunks of time to make follow-up calls, check email, have live meetings, marketing, etc.

7. Catch-all. Get a journal, notebook or pad of paper that serves as your catch-all notebook. Keep messages, phone numbers, thoughts, writings, to-do lists, meeting notes, directions, etc. in one, easy to reach place so you always know where everything is. No more Post-It notes for your To-Do lists or writing messages on scraps of paper. Keep it with you at all times.

8. Shorten your To-Do list. I know this sounds anti-intuitive, but it is very important to limit your to-do list to only 3-5 main tasks or priority activities to complete per day. Having lists too long will keep you stressed out, rushing and unable to truly complete items effectively. This also allows you to keep a comfortable pace throughout the week and not get burned out or overwhelmed.

9. Money/Finances. The first thing to master about money and vision is a deep understanding that your self-worth is not directly attached to your net worth. As you are on this vision path, there may be lean financial times and there will be abundant times. It is critical to master being consistent emotionally in whichever season your vision is experiencing.

Whether you are experiencing a lean time or an abundant time, be a good steward of your money and do not allow yourself to be affected or changed by your bank account balance. God blesses order and you need to demonstrate your ability to be trusted with a little before your overflow can have the space to arrive in your life and business.

This had been my weakness over the years of building my business. I was so busy focusing forward and keeping my eyes on the prize that the daily financial management of things did not always receive the time they deserved. It's time to take a look at your financial records, files and bookkeeping and get them in order.

10. **Office.** Along with your visionary office hours, take some time this week to get your physical space in order. Make sure you have a designated space in which you work so you can always locate files, messages, phone numbers, notes, research, etc. Is your office in order? Is it set up in a way that excites you when you walk into it in the morning? If not, take a few minutes to make some changes that will open up your energy flow and excitement about your office area.

11. Limit Access. This should have been the first one on the list of tools to manage your time. The more you limit access to yourself, the more you get done and empower those around you to grow. Turn off the ringer on the phone, get out of the office, close your door so those around you honor your time. Do whatever you need to limit access to your time. I am reading a book on time management by Dan Kennedy, a multimillionaire who works with affluent business owners, in which he shares that he does not even own a cell phone. He does not accept incoming phone calls or emails. He requires that all correspondence come to him via his fax machine.

The other area to limit in your life is meetings – most of which are unnecessarily long and ineffective. Honor your time with clear boundaries and you will see your effectiveness profoundly increase.

12. Other _____. What other areas need to be brought into order so you feel as ready as possible to operate in your fearlessness?

Can you imagine the difference that getting these areas ready for your new fearless life will make? Challenge yourself, set a timer in small increments of time and see how much you can get done. Block time out in your calendar to get these areas ready. Do a little at a time and you will see an amazing difference in all areas of your life. Keep working on them until they are complete.

Powerful Questions and Inquiries

What areas of your life still need some attention before you are ready to live fearlessly?

_____

_____

_____

_____

_____

_____

What has to change in those areas?

_____

_____

_____

_____

_____

_____

_____

_____

Are there any remaining fears about creating your new and ideal life?

_____

_____

_____

_____

_____

_____

_____

Take a good look at your current friendships. Which friends reciprocate your energy and positivity?

_____

_____

_____

_____

_____

_____

_____

_____

_____

Which "friends" leave you feeling drained and silently frustrated?

_____

_____

_____

_____

_____

_____

_____

_____

_____

What would you change about your significant relationship so it fully supports your vision?

_____

_____

_____

_____

_____

_____

_____

_____

_____

This Week's Exercises

1. Complete your Powerful Questions & Inquiries for this week.

2. Pull out your calendar and take a good look at all of your meetings, appointments and things that take your time. Decide what things cannot be removed, which things will take some time to remove and which things can go immediately. Are you willing to put some of these things on the back-burner until your vision is moving along powerfully?

3. Make a list of any questions or areas of support you need. Make sure you get all of the coaching or support you need to move forward.

4. Please make sure you are fully caught up to this point in the challenge. If not, please set some time aside to get caught up.

The Fearless Living Challenge

Challenge 4: Releasing Emotional Barriers To Fearlessness

Challenge 4

Releasing Emotional Barriers

to Fearlessness

Forty-two years and nine months. That is how long my friend Terry has been dealing with the "reign" of her verbally abusive, emotionally unavailable mother. A mother who kept her dressed up all of the time and seldom showed her anything positive outside of providing money. She was emotionally aloof and 364 days of the year would constantly tell her how worthless she was. On the 365th day, Terry's birthday, she put on an act of being a good mother.

Every year she would throw Terry a wonderfully decorated theme birthday party and made it a point to invite every child in the neighborhood. The kids thougt she was the coolest mother ever! Her mother learned to mask her facade of the perfect mother under pink lacy dresses with matching purses, hats and ankle socks. Anytime outsiders were looking in they saw a mother who must have taken great care of her little girl, yet behind closed doors, she would make it a point to destroy Terry's delicate sense of self.

Last night Terry called me offended by a friend whose interaction reminded her of her mother's emotional bullying, mental manipulation and scornful comments. God brought Terry a message through me and I shared with her the spiritual aspect of what was going on. It was time for her to free herself from the wrath and the forty-two years of damage that her mother had inflicted upon her. Enough was enough. It was time for Terry to break herself loose and begin to see herself for the incredible person she is.

One of my gifts is being an emotional healer. For years I have had the honor of working one-on-one with people ready to break free of the chains and shackles of their past pain and catapult into the future they knew was living inside of them all along. We all have incomplete emotional wounds and baggage that we carry around. The challenge with this emotional baggage is that it gets heavy. Very heavy. As long as you are carrying around your past emotional baggage, you are bound by your past and unable to fully participate in creating the future God created you to live.

It took me years to free myself of my own emotional issues. Growing up in one of the few African-American families in Olympia, Washington came at a high price. It cost me my self-confidence, self-worth and left me feeling unlovable and unattractive. I remember loathing recess because it meant being chased across the school grounds with boys kicking me in the butt yelling, "Big Butt, Big Butt! Blackie, and Thunder thighs." I remember longing to have the same long, straight hair like my friends Robyn, Kelly, Christy, Michelle and Angie. Did I mention Heather?

My family was one of the most well-known families in town because of my father's successful business and my mother being President of The School Board throughout my whole public school education. Yet, my father always worked and was seldom home before bedtime. I don't recall him ever attending a tee ball or softball game, volleyball match, track meet, soccer tournament, or one of my countless speaking engagements – and I was good!

I do not recall my dad ever attending one of the all-student body assemblies that I led every Friday afternoon throughout High School. I remember having to schedule two weeks out for him to attend a special assembly my Senior year. I was competing with 25 other Seniors girls to have the privilege of representing my school as a Princess on the royalty court of Lakefair, the multi-city-wide yearly celebration.

While some young people covered their pain with drugs and alcohol, I covered my pain with my friends and working to be the best in student leadership and on my sports teams. In elementary school, I learned how make up for being overweight by honing my athletic ability so I would never again be the last one left on the wall when teams were chosen in gym class. I did not have a single boyfriend. I did not have the experience of someone taking romantic interest in me until I transferred colleges to Howard University when I was 21 years old. And boy, did I make up for lost time – whew (that's a book in-and-of itself)!

I know it was God keeping me during those

years. Even with all of the issues I was working through, I always knew deep, deep, deep (did I say, deep) down inside that I was destined for greatness and to make a tremendous impact on the world. There was just too much in the way for me to really believe it or experience it in a powerful way. It wasn't until my older sister called me up and invited me to take a transformational emotional breakthrough course during my freshman year in College at my first college, Western Washington University, in Bellingham, Washington.

It was then that I began to allow myself to feel the pain of not having my father present while living under the same roof. I felt like I wasn't good enough, worthy enough, lovable enough or just enough, period. The course assisted me in seeing that each and every one of my emotional issues and challenges was rooted in the painful reality of having an emotionally unavailable father in the midst of growing up in "Lily Whiteville USA."

This Week's Focus: This week is the place in the challenge where you really begin to move your fear out of the way. That's the good news.

The not-so-good news is that once you begin to free the way to live fearlessly and bring out your issues, this can leave you feeing emotionally raw and vulnerable. This is where most classes, workshops, books and CD's stop. These teachings tell you what's possible, help you design your idea life and yet seldom ever walk you through the emotional barriers that are keeping you from moving forward. This week you have the chance to arrive on the other side of your past emotional barriers into fearless living.

This is a critical week in the challenge. Make sure you are all caught up to this point and are taking the time to write out your answers in your book. Remember when I asked you to trust the process at the beginning of the Challenge? This week is all about trusting the process because it can bring up any and all residual issues that are standing in the way.

We are literally in the face of our childhood issues and lies that have kept us bound without even fully being aware of it. This week is the last week that you will have to exist on top of these issues. If you find opening up to these memories are too painful, it is a sign to pick up the phone and call me so I can coach and guide you through it. At the very least, send me an email at info@erickajackson.com.

Did you know it is possible to live without having any negative emotional "triggers?" Imagine living free of any self-worth issues and being in touch with your greatness at every moment in the day. Imagine living with an open heart and no fear of being hurt because you know how to walk yourself back to wholeness. You don't have to be guarded. It is possible. I have done so much work around my emotional "stuff," when it does attempt to rear its ugly head, I know how to walk myself through a step-by-step process.

In those rare moments that you are not feeling great, you can take yourself through *The Steps To Emotional Healing* outlined later in this chapter to get yourself in alignment. After my years of emotional work, I am so happy to be a living example of what is possible in terms of being fully healed emotionally and living in the present.

The Purpose of Your Past

Understanding the purpose of your past is

the key to being able to live fully in the present. Really hear me on this one – you were born for a specific purpose and to make an impact in the world that no one else can. God has allowed you to go through challenges so you are fully equipped to fulfill your vision. *You have gone through what you have gone through so your life can be a living testimony for those God has created you to impact.* Your emotional challenges created the tools and necessary armor to carry out your life's mission and purpose. Period. Without your life's experience, you simply would not be ready and strong enough to see it through.

Understand the reason why emotional pain is allowed in your life is for spiritual reasons. God allows challenges in your life not to keep you hurting or to stifle your growth, but to build character and strengthen you for the journey of living out your purpose and calling. The purpose of emotional pain is not to keep you feeling hurt, used or angry. It is to help you free those whom God sends to you in order to impact their lives.

Without having the experience of filing bankruptcy and repairing your credit, you could not tell others how to do it. If you hadn't had the experience and been delivered from the hurt, violation and anger of a rape, you cannot speak into the lives of others who have been victorious. Cancer. Incest. Sexual molestation. Bankruptcy. Homelessness. Drug addiction. Emotional neglect. Physical abuse. Abandonment. Single motherhood. Divorce. Poverty. Betrayal. Imprisonment. Whatever it is you have been through, these were allowed because within your experience lies clues to your life's purpose and Kingdom assignment.

Your emotional pain did not occur so you can feel unworthy, but so you can grow and lean on God. They did not happen so you can close your heart to love and trust, but for you to learn how to forgive the perpetrator and to love in spite of the challenges.

You are not a victim, you are a victor. Your pain teaches you how to exercise your free will to choose to love again and again because each time you choose to love, you move to a new level within yourself. You grow stronger and wiser and are better equipped and prepared to be a vessel for God's purpose.

If you haven't been taught how to heal your emotional baggage, it can become a barrier to experiencing the fullness of your vision. Without healing, you will eventually get stuck and not be able to move forward until you have dealt with your past pain. This pain also leaves an imprint on your spirit that has to be dealt with simultaneously in the spiritual realm. You carry your emotional baggage around in invisible purses, carry-on bags, suitcases and trunks. You might even have a storage unit of emotional baggage somewhere. Here are explanations of the types of emotional baggage to which I am referring:

Purse –Your own issues of self-worth, doubt, inadequacies, etc.

Your "purse" issues are easy to carry around and aren't easily recognized by others. You can easily tuck them away and they don't really slow you down that much. You can even get a cute purse that matches your outfit. Your purse issues really show up in negative self-talk and gremlins (see below for a full explanation).

Carry-on baggage – Your "carry-on" baggage holds your friendship issues, betrayal, etc.

You know you have carry-on issues if you have experienced challenges that have left you more closed and wounded from friendships that went sour. Trust issues with friendships are also carried around in an emotional carry-on bag. You can even have more than one carry-on bag and still maneuver through life because they only slow you down a bit. You can usually tuck them away under your seat or in the storage bin above your head and get on with the business of your life.

Suitcase – Your "suitcase" represents those past romantic relationship issues.

Now we're getting heavier. Although your past romantic issues or broken hearts seem to be hidden, you unknowingly drag them around in suitcases. You know you have suitcase issues when your heart has been wounded during or after a significant relationship and somewhere along the way you have decided not to fully open up or be as vulnerable with the next person. I am constantly astounded at how many people's hearts are still back in the 1980's or 1990's.

Trunk – Your "trunk" issues are your family, parent, daddy, mommy, childhood issues and residual past programming that keeps you stuck.

Trunks are awkward, too heavy to carry and the metal that covers the corners and edges leaves drag marks behind. If you have past or unhealed issues of anger, abandonment, emotional unavailability, etc., they usually originated from your immediate family when you were a child. After working with hundreds of people on their healing, I have run into only one situation where the daughter grew up in a wonderfully loving household that did not leave her wounded. It was her experiences later in life that led to the demise of her self-esteem and self-love.

Storage Unit – Issues of violation, rape, incest, molestation, etc.

Your storage unit issues are the most challenging to release because they involve being a victim to someone else's past, unhealed issues. Storage units are big and they are kept somewhere separate and out-of-site, therefore, you go to great lengths to keep your stuff behind locked doors. Yet, they are costly! You get a bill every month and it takes a toll on you to keep your stuff under lock and key. These are issues of sexual violation, which can leave very deep wounds and confusion for years to come. Even storage unit issues can be healed following *The Steps To Emotional Healing.*

Fear and Gremlins

At this point in the challenge you may begin saying to yourself "How in the world am I going to make all the money I want to make?", " How will I be able to support myself in my business full-time", or "What if I finish this challenge and fear still stops me from moving forward?" In the coaching world, these self-sabotaging voices that often show up at the most inconvenient times are called *gremlins*, a term coined by Richard Carson.

Your gremlins are residue from your past, unhealed, unreleased and unforgiven emotional issues – your "stuff." It is easy to get caught off guard and have your "stuff" appear out of what seems like nowhere. Negative programming stemming from your past and any remaining self-worth and esteem issues will show up in this phase. Your gremlins present a wonderful opportunity to deal with and complete any unresolved issues.

During this part of the challenge, it is important to give yourself extraordinary support. Spend extra time journaling, sitting quietly, taking baths, exercising, crying or spending time with positive loved ones. If you experience some very deep issues coming up, you may need to seek additional assistance from a professional counselor or therapist. Coaching focuses forward while counseling and therapy can delve deeper and help you identify and release past issues. Coaching can work in great partnership with mental and emotional health professionals.

The important thing to remember is that experiencing these feelings is part of the process and it signals the fact that you are ready to lighten your emotional load, expand your comfort zone and move forward. Remembering this will keep you moving forward without getting stuck in this highly vulnerable phase. You will be amazed at how much you can create when you allow your fears to rise to the surface. Practice surrendering your fear as often as it comes up for you (and it will come up often at first) through prayer and meditation. Identify the name of the fear (fear of success, fear of failure, fear of the unknown, fear of having no friends, etc.) you are feeling and surrender it as often as necessary during your morning prayer and quiet time (hint, hint). Fear will soon be a thing of the past and will never hold you back again.

Working the Gremlin

It is important to let your gremlins (your negative and self-sabotaging thoughts, doubts and fears) know you are no longer willing to maintain the status quo in your life. Your gremlins are dark spiritual forces that can attempt to block you from moving forward and achieving what you truly want. I literally talk to my gremlins to let them know that they will not stop me as I continue to stretch and challenge myself to grow and move forward.

I have several gremlins that appear in my life from time to time. There is the gremlin around men and dating that is rooted in my little girl past of never experiencing being liked back by anyone I had a crush on. Or seeing that I consistently intimidated men and they ended up with a woman of much less character and depth. This took its toll on me over the years. It came to a "head" when the father of my child married another woman while I was three-months pregnant with his child. I found out the night before and had no time to prepare. I cried every night for three months! I named this gremlin, who still appears from time-to-time, Susan.

There is also a gremlin that comes up when I look at the excess weight I have carried since I gave birth to my daughter (she's eleven!). I haven't named that one because I don't want to get too attached. This gremlin whispers to me that I am not slender enough or that I have to lose all of my weight before I can move forward in fully living the life I've worked so to hard to create over the last 11 years against all odds as a single parent.

Gremlins lose their power over you when you identify them for what they are. Notice your options in the situation and then consciously choose what it is you really want. Your gremlins might be, "I am not good enough," "I don't have enough time" or "If I'm really successful, I won't be able to trust anyone." etc.. When your gremlins appear, you can take a moment to silently talk to them and explain why you are good enough, how you will create time or how you will meet new people to trust along the way.

Just be careful that you don't talk out loud in public places to your gremlins. I don't want to be responsible for getting you checked into the nearest psych ward of your hospital. In this age of cell phones, this works great because no one will know you are actually talking to yourself and not on your cell phone as you drive to or from work chatting with your gremlins. In other words, don't take your gremlins too seriously and have fun with them.

The Steps To Emotional Healing

1. Acknowledge that incomplete pain is present.

2. Identify the source of the pain. When did it begin? Who is it associated with? When was the last time you remember not having this emotional pain?

3. Fully realize the depth of the pain you are feeling. When you allow yourself to feel it, how badly does it hurt? Where do you carry the pain?

4. Ask yourself what you made it mean about yourself. What conclusions did you draw about yourself? What did you attach or Velcro to what happened? How are you punishing yourself? How are you sabotaging yourself? Did you make it mean that you aren't good enough or worthy enough?

5. Remember the negative and positive that you experienced. What lessons did you learn? What blessings have come out of the pain?

6. Express your pain. Let it out...bring completion to the situation without doing harm to yourself or anyone else. Go beyond the anger. Write it. Speak it. Scream it (into a pillow or on a walk in the woods).

7. Re-program yourself to redefine your reality. Work on the things that make you feel lovable and deserving of the best. Post what

you really want to internalize and believe on your walls, in your wallet, on your desk and on your dashboard.

8. Pray! Pray! Pray! Take time to get in touch with God and the fact that you are a child of God. Give your burden to God. Release it. Ask God to take the pain from your heart and spirit. He will. You can wake up and no longer have to carry that raw feeling of hurt and pain.

9. Forgive yourself and the other(s) involved. They didn't know better or didn't act on what they know to be right at the time. Even if it appeared that they vindictively or purposely set out to hurt you, they did what they knew to do at the time. They may have even been doing the best they could at the time. Write a letter to every person you have not yet forgiven. Ask a friend to pretend to be that person and listen to all you have to say. Talk it out with yourself. Do what you have to do in a safe way.

10. See it, speak it, be it!!!

You can take any issue still hiding out in your emotional baggage and walk it through these steps and you will be released from it. The best way is to think through the steps and then write them down to get them out. Once you write them down, *do* something with them. Burn them. Tear them up. Bury them. Perform some ritual that represents letting it go. I once even went to a stream, ripped up my steps and watched them go downstream. Do whatever it takes to be emotionally free of your barriers to the fearless life you deserve.

The Art of Forgiveness

Although you can forgive anyone and anything, no matter how painful the experience was, you will not forget. Your power is in being able to remember it without having an emotional reaction. That is when you know you have really forgiven. If the person who did you wrong walked into the room, once you have forgiven them, you will not have a physiological response of tension, anger or nervousness at all. They can no longer touch you. You have taken back your power and you are living for your future. There is nothing they can say or do to negatively affect you anymore.

This is true forgiveness and it is imperative to experiencing your blessings. You will block your blessings to the extent that you have not forgiven. Unforgiveness turns into disease. Fibroids. Cancer. Excess Weight. Bitterness. Anger. Don't allow yourself to be angry and not forgiving another day. It is fully in your power to release the pain.

Powerful Questions and Inquiries

What can your life look like without any remaining emotional barriers?

_____

_____

_____

_____

_____

_____

What emotional barriers are left in your heart?

_____

_____

_____

_____

_____

_____

_____

_____

_____

_____

What emotional baggage are you still carrying?

_____

_____

_____

_____

_____

_____

What negative self-talk are you still dealing with?

_____

_____

_____

_____

_____

_____

Who do you have yet to fully forgive? List their names here:

_____

_____

_____

_____

_____

_____

If you could say anything to each person you have not forgiven, what would you say? (Let it rip!!! You may need more paper for this one.)

_____

_____

_____

_____

_____

_____

_____

_____

_____

_____

_____

_____

_____

_____

_____

This Week's Exercises

☐ 1. Complete this week's Powerful Questions & Inquiries.

☐ 2. Take time to answer each of the questions listed throughout this week's text. Write letters to those you need to forgive. Talk your answers out loud with yourself. Don't keep it in, let it out.

☐ 3. Write a love letter to yourself. Acknowledge yourself for all the things you would love to hear from others or your significant other. Here is the space for your love letter. You can also write yourself a lovely card or put your letter on stationary.

The Fearless Living Challenge

Challenge 5: Embracing Fearless Success

Challenge 5

Embracing Fearless Success

Each week the lessons have easily poured out of me and onto paper. This week, it was different. I had a hard time. I have learned that pushing too hard never works for me. I had to just stop trying to force it and lie down and take a nap. When I woke up, I knew why it was so difficult.

I don't have that much to say about this topic. It's so clear to me. It's just time to open up to and embrace your fearlessness. You've been preparing for it all of your life. You have wanted it. Desired it. It's simply just time. Yes, I have some insights to share, but the basic fact remains the same – it's time to stop wanting and fully embrace all that you know you are ready for.

When I was working to fully embrace

success, I imagined myself standing barefoot on the warm, soft, brown sand of the Pacific Ocean on a summer evening during a breath-taking sunset. With my head thrown back and my skirt blowing in the gentle breeze, I see myself opening my arms as wide as I can and actually trying to let it all in. When I look at the vastness of the ocean, I think of God. This vision represents me taking in all that God has for me.

It really stretches me to imagine taking all of the incredible beauty, opulence, power and joy into my being. That is what embracing fearless success feels like to me. You will have to create your own vision of what it feels like to you and hold on to this vision. Take yourself there any time you feel yourself shrinking or not feeling like you have the space you need to fully bring forth your power to the world.

The current vision I use is me standing on stage after delivering an amazing speech that inspired the entire arena of thousands of people, who have shown up to hear my message, to stand to their feet and holler uncontrollably at the top of their lungs. My arms are opened to the audience crying tears of gratitude for their reaction and to God for blessing me with the privilege of doing this work.

Big Vision, Big Faith

Living out the fullness of God's vision for your life is huge and it takes huge faith to go through the process. Faith is knowing God is keeping His Word and providing for you at all times – no matter what it looks like. Hebrews 11:1 shares with us that *"Now faith is the substance of things hoped for, the evidence of things not seen."* Faith is believing in the essence of what it is you desire and taking action as if it already exists.

Fear and faith cannot co-exist. To live fearlessly means choosing sides. What side are you going to choose? Will you choose fear or faith? Are you going to really live all out in faith and let fear go once and for all? Or are you going to hide behind fear and use it as an excuse for another day?

While we have been taught to think that stepping out on faith is scary and risky, the truth is that it's blissful because it takes you beyond the physical world that is based solely on your five senses to a place that transcends the physical world and is based solely on your five senses. It takes you to a euphoric place that feels like floating. Everything is not perfect all the time, but you can always bring yourself back to your fearless center.

So...it's time to move forward into the fullness of your life. Faith requires action. Stop right now and close your eyes (okay, close them once you read what to do next). Allow yourself to imagine yourself living fearlessly. How would your life change? How would your business change? How would your relationships change? How would being in your skin feel different? Would you talk differently? Would you think differently? What does huge faith look like for you? Take your time and imagine every aspect of your life after crossing the threshold into fearlessness.

This Week's Focus: This week is

about putting your big faith into practice. It's easy to have faith when all is going well in your life. When your bank account looks like you would like it to or when things seem to be going your way, it's easy to be faithful. Fearlessness requires a whole new level of faith that most people aren't willing to experience.

Faith doesn't lie in words, it lies in experience. So, this week is about experiencing your faith at a higher level. I mean that kind of faith when you have no fear and don't know where rent is coming from and it's due at 5 pm the same day. Faith that leaves those around you confused and not understanding because you are willing to step into a new realm of faith.

Say Goodbye To Small

One thing is for sure when it comes to fearlessness – it's time to say goodbye to small ways. No more playing small. No more talking small. No more walking small. No more thinking small. No more accepting anything that resembles small (lack, negativity, procrastination, etc.) in your life, your relationships and in your environment. As I write this, I am asking myself the questions and really getting that every new level you move to requires you to take yourself through these steps again. There will always be areas to grow into.

As you move through your world this week, put on an objective hat and take inventory of the areas of your world in which you are still playing small. As I look around in my world, I see those areas as my bank account and my new townhouse. It just doesn't fit.

I have envisioned a lovely burgundy ultra-suede couch with a chase lounge on the right side and I look and there is an awkward blank space in my living room because the couch is still sitting in the show room of Levitz Furniture. Or when I look at my bank account, I am truly thrown off because I know who I am and what I have to offer the world and I truly believe that there should be a balance no smaller than $1,000,000 right now. Yet, I still experience challenges in my finances and don't have the money I choose to have to live out the fullness of my vision. These are areas in which I am playing small and it's time to bring them into full alignment. I'm ready, are you ready?

Pick an area of your life or a project to demonstrate your faith and begin working on it. That business you've wanted to expand. That book you've wanted to begin. That phone call you've been meaning to make. That research you've been longing to do. That song you have wanted to put onto paper. That product you have had in your heart to create. Pick a project and begin working on it during your visionary office hours.

Powerful Questions & Inquiries

How will dismissing fear from your life change things for you? What will you do differently without the fear? (B-r-e-a-t-h-e on this one, it's a deep question).

_____

_____

_____

_____

_____

_____

In what areas are you still playing small?

_____

_____

_____

_____

_____

_____

_____

_____

This Week's Exercises

- 1. Complete asking yourself the questions I've added in this week's text.

- 2. Complete the powerful questions and inquiries.

- 3. Open yourself to embracing your fearless living. Really walk in it and allow yourself to experience it.

- That's it! You can do it!

The Fearless Living Challenge
Challenge 6: Communicating Fearlessly To The World

Challenge 6

Communicating Fearlessly To

The World

This week is a rather easy week. I want to simply tell you to stand on the highest mountain peak or hill you can find, open your arms and scream, "From this day on, I choose to live fearlessly!!!" But, since it's not quite that easy, I do have a bit of teaching I want to share.

When I started this work, I had to remind myself daily through affirmations and prayer that I was committed to fearless living. I learned to become conscious of the times in which I was playing small or folding down my wings. Now, it isn't even a thought, it just is. I actually laugh to myself often because in my fearlessness, it feels like I am towering over people or floating two inches above the ground moving in my own world. I often look up and find people - especially children - staring at me. I used to think I must have a booger (Is this how you spell that?! I don't even think this is a real word. It's not in the dictionary!) hanging out of my nose.

This Week's Focus: Now that you

have done some incredible work around stepping into your fearlessness, it's time to learn how to posture your fearlessness in the world. While it is ideal to say that you won't have any challenges speaking up and expressing your fearlessness, the truth is that it will take a bit of time to fully integrate it into your language, movement and environment. This week is about learning how to set new boundaries and communicate your fearlessness at all times. You literally have to re-train those around you to give you more space for greatness and to learn how to encourage your fearlessness and not discourage it.

Fearlessness is deeply rooted in true power and people will begin to behave in extremes around you. People recognize power. True power comes from God and people spend lifetimes trying to emulate what they perceive as power, instead of understanding its source. As always, you will attract like-minded people for the most part, but you can also have challenges with people who are intimidated at your power, peace, focus and joy. Your spirit will become sensitive to this, so don't spend too much time thinking about it. The more people you have in your inner circle, the more challenging this can be.

As you move in your fearlessness, people will have one of three reactions to you:

1. Others on God's purpose path will be very drawn to you and want to be around you. (This is very good for business!). This will be the reaction of those individuals who are on the same or a similar path as you. God will illuminate these people so you can recognize them and they will recognize your illumination.

2. Some people still struggling with their issues will be so uncomfortable around you that they will keep a comfortable distance. These individuals will come up with excuses and find a way to dismiss themselves from your presence. These are the people to be most cautious about because they will

have a tendency to be quite negative before they see that they cannot sway or influence you.

However, if you practice the communication techniques that follow, they will either allow their light to shine brighter or they will subtly withdraw from your presence. You will look up one day and realize that you haven't talked to your negative friends and it will be just fine with you because God will send new and wonderful people your way.

3. The last group of people will run in the other direction. This can be baffling if you want these people to stick around. The truth is, they can't. They are in so much fear and trepidation, that without you even opening your mouth, they will be unbearably uncomfortable and avoid you. While this sounds like a bad thing at first glance, the truth is, it saves you so much energy and time wondering if someone can "hang" or not.

While these reactions are wonderful once you fully step into your fearlessness, the transition to getting there can be a challenge. How do you begin to let people know your new fearless lifestyle? The easiest thing to do is to first realize that most people are not going to understand and if you stop expecting them to, it will make your life much easier.

Although I haven't taken an official poll, I would venture to say that less than 3-5% of people truly live fearlessly.

Fearless living ushers you into an elite group of people that move beyond talking about their faith and God to experiencing and exercising their faith. Most people don't understand. The great news is that most people don't have to understand. You only need a few people to partner with you on this journey and everyone else will be blessed by your presence and your life will be the example of what is possible for them.

Creating New Boundaries

A former spiritual mentor of mine used to talk about how we have people on the front rows of our lives and they really need balcony seats. This analogy applies to fearlessness. At this point, you must be clear about your new-found boundaries of operation. Think about what really supports you living fearlessly.

- Do you need more quiet time?
- Are you longing for more sleep?
- Do you need more supportive people around

you?

- Do you need to slow down and have more help around the house?

- Do you need to relax more and have time to read and drink tea?

- Do you need to set aside undisturbed time to work your visionary office hours?

- Do you need more time to read The Word and other inspirational books?

- Do you need time to execute all of the ideas that God pours into you about your business and making more money?

- What do you need to truly be fearless?

Arlene was a client of mine in a three-month coaching program. She was actually a business mentor of mine-turned-client. As we identified her main issues, her husband, Frank, kept coming up. Frank was very negative while Arlene was an incredibly happy and upbeat person. Frank was like that little man in the Gulliver's Travels cartoons who was always saying, "We'll never make it."

Arlene was tired of it and needed to work on communicating her greatness and fearlessness to Frank. She learned how to turn anything he said into a positive and feed it right back to him to neutralize his pessimistic outlook. He was not living his purpose and at first he found it annoying, then as Arlene continued to work her vision, he got in touch with his and crossed over to positivity and support. This transformed their relationship and they now do their vision work of being missionaries traveling around the world together and deeply enjoy each other's company.

I have a low tolerance for negativity or limited thinking. I have learned some great communication techniques to support those around me in lifting the bar of faith and forward movement in their lives. Although you will develop your own language and techniques, here are some great ways I communicate fearlessly with those around me without being too forward, judgmental, or agitating:

- I think it's the coach in me, but if someone shares negativity or talks negatively about themselves or others, at first I listen and then I ask them a question that will make them think, such as, "Is that what really works for you?" or "That's an interesting way to look at it, is there another way that would feel a bit better to you?"

- If I am not in a coaching "space", I will simply will be quiet and not say much of anything. Not in an uncomfortable way, in a way that allows them to hear themselves without my input or enabling.

- When I began this journey to living God's purpose full-time for my life, I only shared it with those that I knew could understand my faith walk.

- I actually suggest to people that they give notice to those around them. Just as you would give notice at a job when you are getting ready to leave, give notice to those around you that your life is about to change and move to new levels. Let them know how it will affect them. Perhaps you have a certain friend that you talk to way too late at night and it affects your ability to get up early enough to get your vision work done. Let that friend know you have made a new commitment to being on purpose and you all will have to shorten your calls and be off the phone by 10:30 pm each night except on Fridays.

- I let the other person talk and get it all out (unless it is feeling draining to me) and then I offer another way to look at it by saying, "Or you can also see it like it is a blessing..." just to break up the energy of doubt and fear they are bringing forth.

- I don't answer the phone nearly as much anymore. I am amazed at how many people have become slaves to the telephone ringer. I actually let go of my voicemail and began using a digital answering machine I had all along to screen my calls for me. The telephone is the doorway to most of the drama in people's lives and you have to remember that you have dominion over the phone and people's ability to impose upon you.

- I let people know what works for me. I remember starting my business and my friends with jobs did not understand that I was 100% responsible for my income and they would call at all times during the day and ask me to do social things during my work days. This boundary really needed to be set with my daughter who thought I did nothing but sit around the house all day. She would call me to bring lunches, homework and gym clothes she forgot that day. I had to learn to say, "No." She sometimes slips on this one, but I quickly let her know that she has to treat my working from home as if I work outside of the home and I couldn't' stop if I worked a typical job. I now remind her to make sure she has everything, because I will not be able to bring it up to the school for her. She miraculously remembers her things almost all the time.

- I keep it light. If I'm chatting with a close friend, I can say to them, "Girl, you KNOW that was wrong, right?" or "You know you sound crazy, right?" in a laughing way and we can laugh about it. They know they can do the same to me.

- When I was in corporate America, I posted positive sayings and affirmations in my cubicle so people would get in the right mindset and not bring their blues into my space.

- When I was in the job-world, my cubicle was the one everyone stopped by, took a seat and wanted to chat at anytime during the day. I could easily spend most of my day listening and sharing wisdom. I had to learn how to let them know when I was available and when I wasn't. I would say, "Sarah, thanks for stopping by. I'm in the middle of a project, can we chat later?" Or "I really want to hear your story, I just don't have time right now. Shall we continue this talk at lunch or break?"

- Smiling keeps a lot of negativity away. Unhappy people look for other unhappy people to make them feel better and if you are smiling, they won't feel that their negativity is welcomed.

- The best way to get someone to stop their train of thought is to call their name. This stops them long enough to hear how they sound and shift to something more uplifting.

- I have always kept affirmations, pictures of what I am attracting and images that inspire me posted around me. Without even opening my mouth, people are uplifted and move into a space of thinking what it is they really want.

- Set up a meeting with your family and/or significant other and let them know what support, positivity or encouragement you need from them. Make sure to ask what they need from you.

- I often correct myself when I allow something not so nice or negative to come out of my mouth. It's to the point where my friends will correct me if I get out-of-hand.

- What are some things that work for you? What would you like to try as you move forward?

While you will find that most people you surround yourself with will simply be uplifted and inspired by your fearlessness and others will shift with little or no effort, applying these tips and techniques will help you communicate fearlessly with others.

Dancing With Others In Your Fearlessness

When you are dancing, both dancers have to be in sync or someone gets their toe stepped on. When one partner changes the step, the other has to follow. Fearlessness is about dancing with others powerfully in the world. It's time to dance on a whole new level. Start at the top. No more starting toward the bottom and working your way up. I call it taking the service elevator to the top.

I challenge you to remember that you are a peer of even the most powerful person you can imagine. Who is it? Someone who has intimidated you in the past or someone you read about or watch on TV who you would love to sit and talk with. Prior to fearlessness, thinking of sitting with this person may have caused your stomach to flip, your mouth to go dry and your hands to begin to ever-so-slightly shake. Practice seeing yourself with them hanging out. What would you say to them? How will the interaction be?

Remember, everyone is your peer. Your boss, that gorgeous man you see at lunch everyday, that wealthy business owner you would like to approach about your business, your Pastor and First Lady, Bill Gates, Susan L. Taylor, Cicely Tyson, Oprah, etc.. There is nothing between you and them except time and being chosen to live your own, unique vision. You are fully comfortable in your skin and it shows. You love who you are and are enamored with who you are becoming. You are so fearless that others are uplifted by your very presence. Even money flocks to you.

Today, release any feelings or lies from your past that told you that others can be on another level than you. It is simply not true. Allow your fearlessness to usher you into experiencing this every single day. Allow God's favor to go ahead of you and give you preferential treatment. Yes, go find your mountain top, stand there looking out over the world, open your arms and yell, "From this day on, I am fearless!!!"

This Week's Exercises:

☐ Complete asking yourself the questions throughout the text.

☐ Complete the Powerful Questions & Inquiries.

☐ Begin communicating your Fearlessness and Greatness on a new level today.

☐ Keep it light and fun! This is the fun part! You will literally make magic in your life and fall in love with watching it unfold in front of your eyes.

Powerful Questions & Inquiries

1. What do you need from those around you to operate in your fearlessness?

_____

_____

_____

_____

_____

_____

_____

_____

2. Have you truly allowed this work to be a reality for you or is something still blocking you from yelling from your mountain top? What is making you hesitate?

_____

_____

_____

_____

_____

_____

_____

3. Who would you most like to be a client, business partner, friend or acquaintance? Try and get your list to at least 10 – Your Top 10. Take a few minutes to design your Top 10 list below:

_____

_____

_____

_____

_____

_____

_____

_____

_____

_____

_____

4. With this being the second-to-last week of The Challenge, is there anything you still need to make this real for you? What is it?

_____

_____

_____

_____

_____

The Fearless Living Challenge

Challenge 7: Walking In Your Greatness

Challenge 7

Walking In Your Greatness

Can I just tell the truth? Writing this week's lesson has been the most difficult. I have been walking around in a prayerful state literally waiting on God to lead me in what to say. Nothing profound and highly transformational is coming through. I suppose this is because I have shared the teachings to assist you in truly living fearlessly prior to this week. So, really, all that is left to talk about is you deciding what it will be like from here on out.

The final reason you may have any remaining fear is because you have not clearly decided what you choose you future to look like. You may fear the unknown because you have not yet decided your future. Although you may have bought into a concept that your future just kind of happens to you and you are just along for the ride. The truth is that you are a co-creator with God and it is up to you. God will bless you in accordance to the desires of your heart. Learn how to recognize and respond to the quiet voice of The Lord and live your life like an offering to God and you simply cannot go wrong. God will lead you every step of the way. You probably already know what your next step should be. I can even count on God to help me know how to maneuver my directionally-challenged self through the streets of a new city.

While I may wear my relationship with God on my sleeve, because God is at the center of my work, there are many times that my Christian walk is quiet and may show up in a quiet prayer when I head to a meeting or a quiet moment in the morning to ask what God would He have me do today to forward His work in my life. I try not to be overly "religious" by reciting scripture and giving unsolicited advice like so many of the old school women of traditional churches I've seen over the years. I believe in just being an example and showing how incredible your life is supposed to be when it is dedicated to God.

Recognizing the Voice of God

You were born with the innate ability to sense the voice of God. You may have heard it called, "intuition, a little birdie" or " a gut-feeling. I heard a friend refer to God's inner wisdom as, "Something told me..." Whatever you are accustomed to calling the urgings of The Lord in your life, know that they are there guiding you everyday. Once you get in to the habit of listening to your deep inner guidance, you can then begin to foster your ability to fully recognize the voice of The Lord.

The challenge is that it is a quiet voice that requires silence and quiet time to recognize. The voice of God will not scream over the voices of self-doubt, drama or chaotic busy-ness. To learn to recognize the voice of The Lord, you must slow down and take time to deliberately listen and read His Word. Learning this skill is imperative to your vision coming forth. Only through consistent quiet time and tuning into your inner wisdom on a regular basis can you identify God's voice from any others. This inner voice leads you in the most efficient ways to complete projects, tells you who to trust and provides insight into people that can only come from

God.

While you may experience God's voice as an audible voice from time-to-time, it usually is an inner voice that comes from a place other than your thoughts. For me, it is like a whispering in my ear. I have honed my skill to know when it is my voice and when it is God's voice. I don't even hesitate to be obedient to this voice because I have story after story that proves that His voice always leads me in the right direction.

This Week's Focus:

This week is the final week of The Challenge and it is really about reviewing the previous lessons and making sure that you've GOT IT! You should really have all of the tools, insights and techniques to never allow fear to slow or stop you again for the rest of your life. Are you there yet? If not, let's connect so I can make sure you have everything you need because your greatness lies on the other side.

Your greatness is all about every aspect of your life reflecting the glory of God. This is something I strive for everyday. I choose for every area of my life to reflect all of God's goodness and mercy. From my body to my checkbook. Greatness is not something you aspire to, it *is* who you are. You walk it, talk it, breathe it. Your greatness is not an affirmation on the wall that you repeat to yourself everyday; it is inside of you and permeates from every cell of your being.

For years I was involved in Washington CASH, a micro-lending organization in Seattle and one of the requirements was that we came together with a team of other business owners every two weeks. For years our team had a mentor, Bob, who was a retired business man who did not hesitate to ask the tough questions and say the things no one else would verbalize.

At the end of every meeting, each of us would go around the table and name the goals and intentions to carry out by the next meeting. I remember one, particular meeting where Bob sat patiently waiting for us to speak our goals and objectives; just then he could not hold his tongue any longer. With his hands wringing together, he blurted out, "I hear everything you all have said about getting ready to get set and I am wondering when you are actually going to go."

There was a stunned quiet around the table

as we had a group, "Aha!" moment. Although Bob is not my official team mentor any longer, he is still my mentor and asks me the tough questions no one else will. In the spirit of my mentor, Bob, the tough question for you is, "Will you really live out the fullness of your greatness and never again allow fear to be part of your reality? Are you really going to do it?

Today And Beyond

As you move through your life from today and every day henceforth, it is about feeling, being and expressing your greatness in all of its glory. Take a look around you, what areas of your life feel great? Which areas feel not-so-great? Which areas do you need growth to *live* your greatness? Life is all about letting your greatness come out to play in a big way. You were attracted to this course because you were ready when you began this course 6 weeks ago. You are ready. You are set. It's beyond time to be ready, it's time to go!

Next Steps

It's time to be bold and take action that most people would not be willing to make. It's time to pick up the phone and make that call to connect with that ideal client. It's time to really set aside the time you really need to make your business the highly successful enterprise you have always seen for yourself. It's time to dust off your dancing shoes, put them on and allow each muscle in your body to remember how it used to move so gracefully and powerfully across the dance floor. It's time to look beyond your current circumstances and live deeply and fully with spice. Imagine that beginning today, you are creating a life that people will look at and want to read about for years to come.

Welcome to Fearlessness!

Powerful Questions & Inquiries

What does the voice of God sound like to you?

_____

_____

_____

_____

_____

_____

When have you known that God's voice was speaking to you?

_____

_____

_____

_____

_____

What bold actions will you take to create your ideal life? What is the first bold thing you will complete?

_____

_____

_____

_____

_____

How has completing this challenge changed your life? (Please share your answer to this question with me at info@erickajackson.com. I would love to hear your response.)

_____

_____

_____

_____

_____

_____

_____

What do you choose your life to be like from this day forward?

_____

_____

_____

_____

_____

_____

_____

_____

_____

_____

_____

_____

_____

_____

_____

_____

_____

What else do you need to truly embody this work?

_____

_____

_____

_____

_____

_____

_____

In Closing

Congratulations on completing this Challenge. Thank you for trusting me and opening up to concepts that may have been new for you. I am so excited to hear how this work supports your grander life vision and assists you in living out the fullness of God's vision for your life. My heart goes out to you and I look forward to accompanying you on the rest of this journey.

Please email me and let me know how I can continue to support you. Here's to your amazing life!

With All My Heart, Ericka

The End of this book...the beginning of something wonderful.

Ericka's Special Offers

and Resources

I Am Here For You...

Above all, know that I am here for you. Please don't hesitate to pick up the phone and call me at (919) 954-8005 or email me at info@erickajackson.com. I really worked to put all that you need within this challenge. If, for some reason, you feel like you need further support and assistance.

I will also be premiering new offerings, of which you will be able to receive discounted rates and memberships. I will be specific when I announce them and you can take advantage of those offers when they come out. Also, please make sure you have signed up for my monthly e-zine (electronic magazine) at www.erickajackson.com to stay abreast on upcoming offers.

Please check my website often as I add new tools and resources weekly to help further your vision-journey. www.erickajackson.com.

Other Books by Ericka D. Jackson

Self-Coaching: Your Guide to Living Inside the Bull's-eye, 3rd Edition

The Power of Vision: Recognizing God's Call

Leave Your Job in 2007! : A Step-by-Step Plan to Live God's Vision as Your Full-time Vocation

About The Author

Ericka D. Jackson

Nothing makes Ericka's eyes sparkle like the possibility of people living God's Vision for their lives. She truly understands that achieving success originates with and follows God. Only once you deeply understand your assignment in God's Kingdom, will you begin to experience authentic success. She skillfully blends spiritual insights with practical knowledge that walk you through the process of fully surrendering and clearing away anything in the way of knowing and acting on God's path for your life. She has been gifted with the ability to "see" others' life purposes and visions and to discern what is needed to move them to the next level.

She uses her gifts and experience as a speaker, emotional healer, fearlessness teacher, time manager and entrepreneur to guide others in living God's vision as their vocation. Ericka's life experience and passion for evoking the best out of others naturally evolved into launching The Convergence Center in 2001, a company on a mission to lead a cutting-edge, multi-media movement that provides Christians with the tools, insights and processes for *achieving* personal and professional freedom.

She has developed several teaching series including The Success Salon®, Bigger! Bolder! Better: Taking Your Business to New Heights® and The Ericka Jackson Show®. She is the author of Self Coaching: Your Guide to Living Inside the Bull's-eye, The Fearless Living Challenge: A 49- day Course To Living Your Greatness, Leave Your Job in 2007! A Step-by-Step Plan to Live God's Vision as Your Full-time Vocation and The Power of Vision: Recognizing God's Call. She is advancing in ministry currently as a licensed Evangelist. Ms. Jackson continues to share her gifts, talent and expertise with ministries around the country. She lives in Raleigh, North Carolina with her daughter.